Out on Good Behavior

Teaching math while looking over your shoulder

Barry Garelick

First published 2021
by John Catt Educational Ltd,
15 Riduna Park, Station Road,
Melton, Woodbridge IP12 1QT UK

Tel: +44 (0) 1394 389850

4600 140th Avenue North,
Suite 180,
Clearwater, FL 33762
United States

Email: enquiries@johncatt.com
Website: www.johncatt.com

ISBN: 978 1 913622 44 2

Set and designed by John Catt Educational Limited

REVIEWS

"Armed with a mountain of knowledge (and his now infamous 1960's Dolciani textbook), Barry has written a captivating read. At times humorous and always meaningful, "Out on Good Behaviour" has something that appeals to everyone.

Tara Houle, Founder WISE Math BC, mum, parent advocate.

"The funny and heartfelt anecdotes in this volume succeed in (1) assuring skeptical and initiative-weary educators that they are not alone, (2) suggesting clever arguments to help those educators challenge some currently shiny shibboleths, and (3) modeling, through Garelick's school-level examples, how to remain focused on kids' success through all the noise.

Eric Kalenze, author of "Education is Upside Down" and "What the Academy Taught Us"

"Barry Garelick is the breath of fresh air which reminds me that I am not alone on this planet. Teaching secondary math today can feel isolating when all of the current edu-fads fly in the face of what I have experienced – as a student, a teacher, and a parent. He writes with an indomitable spirit that is his legacy. Bravo!

Joye Walker, high school math teacher in Iowa City Public Schools

ABOUT BARRY GARELICK

Barry Garelick, a second-career math teacher in California. He has written articles on math education that have appeared in the Atlantic, Nonpartisan Education Review, Education Next, Education News and AMS Notices. He is also the author of three books on math education

ACKNOWLEDGMENTS

The chapters in this book originally appeared at the Truth in American Education website (https://truthinamericaneducation.com/) in different form. The author wishes to thank Shane Vander Hart for hosting the series, and J.R. Wilson for patiently making changes at the last minute.

The names of all people in this book, as well as the names of the two schools where I taught, have been changed.

ABOUT THE COVER AND THE ILLUSTRATIONS IN THIS BOOK

The cover of this book is a facsimile/homage to the textbook *Modern Algebra: Structure and Method*, whose lead author was Mary Dolciani. The book was first published in 1962 and went through many reprints and revisions. It had widespread use in high schools in the 60's through the 80's and is regarded by many students who used the book, as well as teachers who taught from it, to be the best algebra book ever written. When it was first written, it was at a time when the U.S. was entering the space race, computers were increasingly becoming part of daily life, and the need for learning mathematics was evident for many students. It features as a kind of character in the story you are about to read.

Many of the illustrations in this book were inspired by drawings that the author's students at St. Stephens did in the spirit of helping their teacher launch his book. The author wishes that the original drawings could have been used, but extends his heartfelt thanks for the efforts and spirit put forth by the following students: Amy B., Braylon H., Isabel C., Jack B., Jazmin V., Nicholas M., Sophia F and Spencer A. He also thanks all of his students at both Cypress and St. Stephens for their hard work and for helping to make him a better teacher.

CONTENTS

INTRODUCTION AND DEDICATION

I am a teacher who writes books about math education. This is my fourth. Teaching math is my second career in what would be retirement for most people. I've taught in various capacities for eight years, five of which have been as a teacher and not as a substitute or assistant.

I want to share some advice I received from Ellen, one of my two "parole officers" whom you will meet in this book. You will find out what I mean by the term *parole officer*, but for now I want to focus on what I was told, which was intended to be helpful:

"Students have more faith in something they think they came up with than something the teacher tells them."

Her advice summarizes what many teachers are taught about how to teach math effectively. In my short career I have met teachers who take this to heart and refrain from answering students' questions directly. Instead, for even the simplest question a student may ask, some teachers respond by playing "read my mind/discover the answer yourselves" games as a way to lead the student to solve a problem on their own.

Some teachers have told me that they are not allowed to answer a student's question directly. In fact, the quote from Ellen was her response to my question of why it's acceptable for students to show other students how to do a problem, but it's not acceptable if a teacher does so. Having students work in small groups rather than the dreaded desks in a row supposedly ensures that there will be collaboration (one of several 21st century skills) and discovery. In the case of math classes, although there may be some of that happening in small groups, it is more likely the case that a student may answer the question at hand that the teacher will not answer. It is also likely that the answer may be wrong.

From time to time, however, most, if not all, teachers will answer a student's question by telling them what they need to know in order to solve a problem. And most, if not all, teachers (myself included) feel guilty doing this, because we are taught that that's giving away the answer and we are handing it to the student, or to put it in more educational terminology: "teaching by telling."

I disagree with this and many other accepted doctrines of education and have written about my views in three previous books. This book is no exception.

Given that my views are not exactly aligned with the educational status quo, I have been asked whether my books threaten my employment in schools. A more pertinent question would be "Does anyone read your books in the schools where you teach?"

The answer is "Very few." In general, teachers who write books or give talks at conferences, unless they are known celebrities in education circles, are viewed as just another education expert in a field overgrown with them. The market is flooded with books about math education. Teachers are besieged with advice from education specialists and consultants promoting themselves and are bombarded on the internet by expert advice—some good but much of it wretched.

Ironically, despite teachers' resentment of the plethora of educational advice, many buy into the buzzwords and edu-fads, including "growth mindset," "grit," "critical thinking," "21st century skills," "collaboration," "creativity," and "open-ended questions are better than problems with one right answer." They also accept the disdain for teaching by telling, desks in rows, teacher at the front, and direct instruction.

Younger teachers have been taught in ed school to accept as valid many of the edu-fads and buzzwords. Older teachers somewhat buy into it but have enough experience that, in the end, allows them to do things like teach at the front of the room using explicit and direct instruction and answering students' questions directly.

I keep my books in plain sight on a bookshelf in my classroom. Students are intrigued with having a teacher who has written books, but they are not interested enough to want to read any of them. One student, a seventh grader, asked if he could borrow one. I gave him *Confessions of a 21st Century Math Teacher*. I saw that he always had the book with him, so I asked him if he had read any of it. "No," he said. "I just like carrying it around with me."

Being a teacher who writes books, then, is more a state of grace than anything else. Which is good because then I don't have to defend my various stances to people who may disagree. I try to blend in and work toward the common goal of educating our students.

To that end, as a teacher it is important to try to get along despite our varying and sometimes disparate beliefs—which I suppose is one of the messages of this book. Another is that we never really know what's going on, although we may have our theories. A third comes from the first math teacher I ever subbed for. We have become friends over the years, and when I finally got my first job teaching, he gave me what he called sage advice: "Tell the administration what they want to hear, then do what is best for your students."

I have been fortunate enough to work in schools where I've been given the autonomy to teach as I wish. I recognize, however, that there are teachers who are not allowed to do so and must conform to mandated practices with which they disagree and that are ineffective. It is to these teachers that this book is especially dedicated.

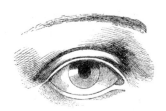

CHAPTER 1

VARIOUS NARRATIVES, GROWTH MINDSETS, AND AN INTRODUCTION TO ONE OF MY PAROLE OFFICERS

If you are reading this, you have either never heard of me and are curious, or you have heard of me and have likely bought into my "narrative" of math education. I tire of the word *narrative* almost as much as *nuance*, both of which I see in just about everything I read nowadays. I thought I'd charge both words rent, since it seemed appropriate for describing all that follows.

I am on a second career as a math teacher, having retired from a forty-year career in the environmental field. I went to ed school at night while I was working, did my student teaching after I retired, and, once I obtained my credential, headed out for the territories.

I am currently teaching seventh- and eighth-grade math at St. Stephens, a small K–8 Catholic school in a small town in California. Prior to that, I taught seventh- and eighth-grade math for two years at Cypress School, another small K–8 public school in another small town in California, which is where I will start this particular narrative.

The Cypress School is in a one-school district, so superintendent and principal were always close by. After receiving praise from the superintendent both formally and informally during my second year there, I received a layoff notice. Such notices are common in teaching, with the newest teachers receiving such notices and usually getting hired back in the fall. Nevertheless, mine was final.

It is tempting to make my termination fit various narratives pertaining to the kind of teachers the teaching profession would like to see less of—specifically, teachers like me who choose to teach using explicit instruction; who believe that understanding does not always have to be achieved before learning a procedure; who post the names of students achieving the top three test scores; and who answer students' questions rather than attempting to get them to a "deeper understanding" by discovering the answer themselves. However logical, compelling and righteously indignant such a narrative might be, my termination will have to remain a mystery and subject to an axiom that applies to teaching as well as many other professions: "You never really know for sure what's going on."

I realize that the praise I received at Cyprus might have represented people seeing what they wanted to see which was often different than what my students saw. For example, I once told my eighth-grade algebra class that my classroom is one place where they won't hear the words "growth mindset"—to which the class reacted with loud applause. Someone then asked what my objections to "growth mindset" were. I said I didn't like how it was interpreted: Motivational clichés like "I can't do it…yet" supposedly build up confidence leading to motivation and ultimately to success. I believe it's the other way around: success causes motivation more than motivation causes success.

Whereas students frequently see through ineffective educational fads, people in education—after buying into such theories—see what they want to see. So when asked by higher-ups or in job interviews how I describe my teaching, I respond: "I provide my students with the necessary instruction to achieve success, which leads to motivation and engagement, and…." It doesn't matter what follows after "motivation and engagement." Those are the magic words that provide the "look and feel" of growth mindset thinking even though it's the opposite of the usual interpretation. In fact, there are many things you can do to make it look as if you're on board with progressivist teaching—if asked.

And I was asked—by my mentors. In California, new teachers must undergo a two-year "induction" program with a mentor with whom teachers meet once a week. The end result of the two-year inquisition is that one's teaching credential is changed from preliminary to permanent. Failure to do this within a certain amount of time means you don't have a license at all. So, it is a rather important process.

I had two different mentors for each year I was at Cypress. I've come to think of them as parole officers who ensure that the newly released prisoners from ed school adhere to the bad and ineffective practices taught there.

I had met with my first mentor, Ellen, a few months before my first year at Cypress began. She was a woman in her 60s who had taught high school biology for thirty years. At our first meeting, she talked about what is involved with math education and the topic of math anxiety.

"I want to give you one piece of advice about math," she began.

I somehow knew this wasn't going to be pleasant.

"Students should do math not only in the classroom, but outside; give examples of real-world problems. Many students dislike math because they find it irrelevant." As a final proof to this statement, she added that it is common for adults to say, "What on earth did I learn algebra for?"

I let a few minutes pass as she talked further about relevance. I then said that in my experience with word problems, or any kind of problem, the relevance to real life never mattered to me. "The usefulness of algebra always seemed evident," I said.

"That's probably because you liked math and had an interest in it and therefore had an inclination to learn it. But there are some kids who, for whatever reasons, hate it and have a hard time with it." It was clear she had given this "you're the exception" argument before.

The particular narrative that she was weaving came back to me often during my second year at Cypress, because it closely matched the seventh-grade class that I taught then. They were a highly discouraged group of students with significant deficits in their math education. I mention them now because a few days after school let out after my second year, I ran into someone who knew those students. He had heard about my being let go, expressed his regrets, and then said, "You must know this. Your students love you. They tell me that they really learned a lot about math and that you were the best math teacher they ever had."

I tell you this anecdote in the hope that as you read this book you obtain a "deeper understanding" of any narratives or nuances thereof that you wish to apply.

Chapter 2

AN ESPRESSO-BASED JOB INTERVIEW, A 1962 ALGEBRA BOOK, AND PROCEDURES VERSUS UNDERSTANDING

In my remaining two weeks at Cypress, I applied for the few math teaching positions that were advertised. I had the typical non-responses except for one—a high school that specialized in problem-based learning. I had applied there out of desperation, never expecting a response. I received an email saying they were interested in interviewing me. Despite my skills at making my teaching appear to be what people wanted to see, I knew that this one would require too much suspension of disbelief.

I canceled the interview saying something along the lines of having to wash my hair that day. Shortly after that, I received another email from the principal at

St. Stephens. They were looking for a part-time math teacher. A fellow math teacher from another school had put in a good word for me. Like the school where I had been, St. Stephens was also part of a small community and had about two hundred students.

A few days later I was at the school for a 2 PM interview. I tend to get a bit logy in the afternoon so I thought I'd have an espresso prior to coming in. The principal, Marianne, and assistant principal, Katherine, interviewed me and asked the usual questions: What does a typical lesson look like, what are my expectations, and so on. My inner voice tried to keep me from extended caffeinated responses. I emphasized how I leave time for students to start on homework in class, do the "I do, we do, you do" technique, and in my controlled ramblings managed to get across (with my heart open and no secrets hidden) that I am, by and large, traditional.

But when the assistant principal asked me what my approach was in teaching algebra, the espresso kicked in big time and my inner voice was having a hard time keeping up. I said that I taught using a 1962 algebra textbook by Dolciani.

Inner voice: "You shouldn't have said that."

"I bought about fifteen of them over the internet when they were selling for one cent apiece about three years ago. So I was basically paying for shipping. But now the prices increased because of Amazon's supply and demand algorithm, so they're selling for about $60 a copy last time I looked. Which tells me a lot of people are buying them."

"Please shut up."

I talked about how I liked the sequence, structure, and explanations of Dolciani's book much better than the official textbook. As it turned out, so did the students despite the increased amount of word problems—and the word problems were yet another plus for using the book.

"But did you cover what was in the Common Core standards?" Marianne asked. I assured them that I did, supplementing with topics that weren't in Dolciani, like exponential growth and decay.

"Good."

I hastened to add that I did not spend inordinate amounts of time on exponential growth and decay functions.

"Idiot!"

"Did you cover exponents at all?" Katherine asked. "Because students generally are weak on those."

"You mean like products and quotients of powers? Oh yeah, big time. The Dolciani book is very big on those." I was about to repeat that I didn't spend much time on exponential growth and decay, but the caffeine was mercifully wearing off.

They did not seem perturbed by any of my ramblings. Then again, it was during the last week of school and I imagine that they were so exhausted that they were probably amenable to anything I said.

They asked about my classroom management techniques. In any interview or evaluation process, one has to have some weakness to talk about and I freely admitted that classroom management is not my strong suit. I mentioned that my seventh-grade math class had behavior problems even though there were a total of 10 students in the class.

"How did you handle the problems?" Marianne asked.

"I had a warning system; two warnings and they got a detention. I wasn't too faithful in carrying that out, though."

"Why was that?"

"When I gave a detention, the two main troublemakers were really good at carrying on about it and crying."

"My major goal was to get them over their feelings of failure." I explained how this group had large deficits in math skills and most of the boys in the group had given up on believing they could learn math.

"How did you do that?" Marianne asked.

"I used an alternative textbook, which my school let me use: *JUMP Math*. It was developed in Canada and broke concepts down into very small incremental steps. It scaffolds problems down to incremental procedures and builds on those."

I went on about how procedures can lead to understanding and you can teach understanding until the cows come home, but most students are going to grab onto the procedures.

"Did it work?" Katherine asked.

"Filling in their deficits definitely helped them; it built up confidence." (I almost said it gave them a growth mindset, but decided against it.)

No more was said; the usual niceties then followed and the interview was over.

They called my references, as well as the principal of Cypress School as I found out the next day. "Marianne called me about you. She sounded excited," the principal told me.

"What did she ask?"

"She wanted to know more about the seventh-grade class; she was curious about their behavior."

"Oh," I said. "I thought she might."

"I told her they were really a tough bunch of students but you handled them well."

"Did she ask about the algebra books I used for my algebra class?"

"No; just about the seventh-grade class," she said.

"How about procedures versus understanding?"

"I don't recall that she did. She sounded positive."

And a few days later I was offered the job at St. Stephens.

"I think you'll like it there," the Cypress principal told me.

I hoped so. There are always doubts about starting any new job, particularly in teaching. I had given them fair warning in the interview about how I taught. I hoped I would be allowed autonomy, but for the most part, I was glad they brought me in out of the rain.

CHAPTER 3

UNDERSTANDING, AND OUTLIERS IN
A SEA OF OUTLIERS

That fall, I started teaching at St. Stephens. I had three classes: the non-accelerated seventh and eighth grade math (Math 7 and Math 8) and eighth grade algebra. During my second week of school, the principal, Marianne, called me in to her office to tell me some good news. "I just want to let you know that we heard from Mary's mother and that Mary said she is really happy in your class; she says that "Mr. Garelick really wants us to understand.""

I was glad to hear that Mary's mother was pleased, but while I haven't taught for very long I knew that I was not any kind of miracle worker. One year earlier at the Cypress School, during back-to-school night a parent of one of my students in my seventh-grade class said something similar. "My son said that this is the first time in any math class that he actually understood the math."

In both cases, it didn't hurt that the word *understand* was used in conjunction with my teaching, although the word has a different meaning for me than what others in education think it means. I want students to be able to do the math. That's pretty much what students mean when they say they understand. Conceptual understanding is important for sure, but it isn't something I obsess over.

Mary was one of two girls in my eighth-grade math class (Math 8) who had to come in twice a week for intervention help for 30 minutes before classes began. The other student was Valerie, who had been classified as special needs since the lower grades. They were both very animated girls; Mary was outgoing and friendly with me. Valerie was more guarded. In her world of smartphones, songs, and reality TV, I felt she viewed me as frightfully out of touch with what was really important. Math was certainly not on her list.

My Math 8 class was similar in some ways to my previous year's seventh-grade class at Cypress –a class acutely aware that they were in the non-accelerated class and who considered themselves "the dumb class." Like my seventh grade math class at Cypress, my Math 8 class at St. Stephens was segmented from the rest of the eighth graders who were in the eighth-grade algebra class (which I was also teaching). During the first week, a rather stubborn and outspoken student, Lou, stated what the rest of the class was feeling: "It's obvious we're not too good at math, which is why they put us in this class."

Compounding the difficulty of a class in which the students already doubted their abilities, Mary and Valerie felt they were not on par with the rest of the Math 8 class—outliers in a sea of outliers. I worked with them as best as I could. I called on them infrequently in the main class and focused on them during my intervention time.

At first, I tried to get them up to speed with what the rest of the class was doing. During one of my sessions with them, I went over one-step equations. I asked them to solve the equation $6x = 12$. I had reached the point where neither one was trying to subtract the 6 from $6x$ to isolate x. But while Mary understood that $6x$ meant 6 multiplied by x, Valerie could not see that. Nor could she see that solving it meant undoing the multiplication by division.

"How do we solve it?" I asked. "How do we undo multiplication?"

"You put the 6 underneath both sides," Valerie said.

That is: $\dfrac{6x}{6} = \dfrac{12}{6}$

Putting one number underneath another meant divide to Valerie which is as procedural-minded as you can get. If ever pressed to justify my acceptance of her level of understanding to well-meaning "doing math is not knowing math" types, I could say that her method at least incorporated the concept that a fraction means division. No one ever asked, but just to make sure I said, "And what do we call the operation when we put one number 'underneath' another?"

She thought a moment.

Mary whispered in Valerie's ear: "Division."

"Oh; it's division," Valerie said.

Over the next few weeks, I worked with the two girls privately while trying to keep them on track in the Math 8 class. I realized that their deficits were so significant that to hold them to the standards of Math 8 would result in failure. Katherine, the assistant principal, agreed with me and said to focus instead on filling in the gaps and to base their grade on their mastery of those.

I leveled with them one morning when they came in for their intervention.

"The Math 8 class must be extremely painful for you," I said.

Valerie let down her guard. "I just don't understand what's going on."

I found her statement true in a number of ways. One was just the fact that she admitted it. But more, it brought home the issue of understanding. Of course she didn't understand—she barely had the procedural and factual tools that would allow her even the lowest level of understanding of what we were doing.

Although there are those who would say "Of course they didn't understand; traditional math has beat it out of them," such thinking is so misguided that, in the words of someone whose name I can't remember, "it isn't even wrong." In the case of Valerie and Mary, they needed more than the two half-hour interventions every week. They needed someone who specialized in working with what is known as dyscalculia. But qualifying as a special needs student doesn't guarantee the student will get the kind of help to deal with a disability.

They had finished what I gave them to do early that day, and Mary—being in a celebratory mood—said the two were going to make a drawing for me. They giggled while they drew a rather strange looking bird laying eggs and eating blueberries, among other odd things going on, and presented it to me. I put it on the wall where it remained for the entire school year. Sometimes, other students would ask what the drawing was, and Mary and Valerie would explain it excitedly. The excitement was partly due to them having drawn it and partly due to my keeping it on the wall for all to see.

Chapter 4

THE PAROLE OFFICER'S CHECKLIST,
THE DIALECTIC OF COMPETITION,
AND GNARLY PROBLEMS

During my two years at Cypress, I had completed the compulsory Teacher Induction Program (TIP) under two different mentors/parole officers. The TIP process consisted of discussions, observations, and the mentors/parole officers filling out an online checklist of items that would serve as the final authentication of my having gone through the induction process.

My first mentor, Ellen, told me that she would be making suggestions and giving me ideas but I was under no obligation to follow any of them. This was good because she had no shortage of dubious ideas and quickly learned that I was going to do things my way. At one point early in our meetings, having determined that I didn't assign group work and rarely had activities, Ellen asked "What are you going to do about Common Core, which requires activities and group work in teaching math?"

"The Common Core standards do not mandate pedagogical approaches. It says so on their website." I expected an argument, but instead she quickly moved on to other business. The mentors are used to teachers fresh out of ed school who are in their twenties and believe whatever they've been told about how to teach and what Common Core requires. In any event, my response remained unrecorded on the online checklist.

My second mentor, Diane, was assigned during my second year at Cypress. Like Ellen, Diane also had teaching experience—second grade, mostly—and was now in charge of the mentor/parole program for the entire county. Like Ellen, she would make suggestions that I could either follow or ignore. She would occasionally evince educational group-think that passed as sound advice.

My first meeting with Diane took place in my classroom. "Tell me about your classes," she said.

I had two that year: a seventh-grade math class (with students who were acutely aware they were in the non-accelerated as opposed to the accelerated class) and eighth-grade algebra—the latter made up of students I had taught the previous year.

"My seventh-grade math class had a rough year last year so they're coming in with an 'I can't do math' attitude right at the start," I said.

"That's never a good thing," she said.

"And on top of that, they have significant deficits. Like not knowing their multiplication facts."

Her eyes widened. "Really? How can that be?"

Actually, it can be and is in many schools across the U.S. I wondered how on Earth she could not know this, being in education as long as she had.

"So how are you addressing that?" she asked.

"I'll let you in on a secret," I said. She looked intrigued.

"I've been giving them timed multiplication quizzes every day to start off the class. My principal told me that timed quizzes stress students, but these kids love the competition; plus, I show them how their scores are increasing."

"Of course!" she said. "Kids love to compete." I was heartened at this for two reasons. She wasn't against memorizing multiplication facts, and she appeared to be going against the education dialectic of "competition is bad." But then she added, "It isn't good to do that in the first and second grades because it can stress kids out, but it's perfect for seventh graders." A few minutes later when I told her I posted the top three scores on quizzes or tests, the dialectic clicked in more fully.

"Are you sure that's a good thing to do? Some of the students who didn't make the top scores might feel left out," she said.

"They ask me who got the top scores, and they don't seem upset when I post them, so I'm assuming it's okay," I said. Her response to this was "I like the way you've set up your classroom," which I took to mean the conversation about posting top scores was over.

Diane liked various quotes I had tacked up on my walls; random things uttered by my students that I felt worthy of posting. Like "I never get used to math; it's always changing" and "Variables don't make sense and make sense at the same time."

I kept the ones from my previous year's classes on the wall, as well as those from my current students. "Seeing quotes from previous classes gives students a sense of legacy and tradition," I said. I pointed out one quote from a student named Jimmy in my current seventh-grade class. It had emerged from a dialogue I had with him on subtracting negative numbers:

Me: You lose 5 yards on a play. You have to make a first down. How many yards do you have to run?

Jimmy: Couldn't you just punt it?

Jimmy had had a particularly rough time in math the previous year and had very little confidence. The first time we had a quiz, I made sure that the students would do well, giving them lots of preparation. Jimmy did do well: 97%. When I was handing back the quizzes, he kept saying, "I know I failed it." When he saw his quiz, he was silent and then asked if anyone in my class last year had failed.

"No," I said.

"Do you think it's possible that I'll pass this class?" he asked.

"Yes, it's entirely possible," I said.

I told Diane about this. "Fantastic that he got 97%. How did that happen?"

I explained how I was using JUMP this year and how it breaks things down into manageable chunks of information that students could master. "They really need to feel a sense of success, given where they were coming from," I said.

"Are you planning to go beyond just mastery and give them some gnarly problems?"

I was tempted to ask her to define "gnarly problems," although I'm fairly sure it had something to do with "If they can't apply prior knowledge to new problems they haven't seen before, there is no understanding." But my answer to her was "Of course." I made a note to myself which when roughly translated was something like, "Come up with something."

JUMP does in fact provide extension problems in the teacher's manual. Given the deck I had been handed with this class, I had other things on my mind besides giving the class gnarly problems, however those were being defined.

CHAPTER 5
THE RITUALS OF SCHOOL, AN UNUSUAL
COMMUNION, AND THE VAST WASTELAND
OF MATH 8

Starting at a new school requires learning a new set of rituals—St. Stephens had many. Each day at St. Stephens began with the entire school of 200 students, plus teachers, gathered around the flagpole to say one or two prayers, sometimes a Gospel reading, and the Pledge of Allegiance. I enjoy the ritual, particularly seeing everyone—first graders through eighth—cross themselves in unison. Before I started at St. Stephens, a friend asked me if knew how to cross myself. "Yes," I said. "But at this point it's procedural; I think the understanding will come later."

My days were built on a set of procedures resulting in an ever-changing understanding of where I stood with my students. After "flag" came the walk to my classroom, walking fast to stay ahead of the rapidly dispersing horde of students. I called my classroom "The Batcave," partly because my classroom is out of the way and cavelike, and partly because that's what I called my classroom at Cypress.

The Batcave at St. Stephens appears to have been a storage closet in a former life and is right next door to the gym. I squeezed eight desks in the room to accommodate the students in Math 7 and 8. It connects to the gym via a set of double doors that get bumped by stray basketballs and other objects. In addition to the bumps on the door, there was also the music played during exercises and dance which usually sparked discussion among my students about the songs being played. I wouldn't change it for the world.

The Math 8 class was held after the Math 7 class. It was the first time I had taught Math 8. I was rapidly discovering that the course was a vast wasteland of disparate topics that outside of basic equations did little to prepare them for algebra in the ninth grade.

After my Math 7 and 8 classes came my algebra class—held in Katherine's classroom because there were sixteen students. Like most of the algebra classes I've taught, this one was full of energetic and motivated students. They were also quite noisy and extremely competitive. The difference between the two classes was never more obvious than when I showed a magic trick to both classes.

It was on a day in which school was dismissed at noon (another cherished tradition in which one's best plans and schedules written over the summer start to resemble a game of Battleship—a day you thought you'd have for a complicated lesson turns out to be a short one). I had performed this trick many times over the years, starting when I was a substitute.

Given the following five cards, someone picks a number from 1 through 31, writes the number on the board and erases it after everyone has seen it so everyone but me knows the number.

On five mini-whiteboards labeled Cards 1 through 5, I had the following numbers written:

Card 1					Card 2					Card 3					Card 4					Card 5			
1	3	5	7		2	3	6	7		4	5	6	7		8	9	10	11		16	17	18	19
9	11	13	15		10	11	14	15		12	13	14	15		12	13	14	15		20	21	22	23
17	19	21	23		18	19	22	23		20	21	22	23		24	25	26	27		24	25	26	27
25	27	29	31		26	27	30	31		28	29	30	31		28	29	30	31		28	29	30	31

I then ask what cards the person sees their number on. I immediately tell them the number. My Math 8 class was quietly amused, showing mild curiousity as to how it was done. I told them (and will tell you in a moment) I asked if anyone wanted a set of business-card sized versions of the trick which I had printed up, so they could perform the trick for others. Only one person asked, the bell rang, and they departed quickly.

I repeated the presentation for the algebra class but embellished it by having them help me construct a table of binary numbers from 1 through 31 and then transfer the information onto the five mini whiteboards to make the five magic cards. Below is what the finished table looked like.

	16	8	4	2	1
1	0	0	0	0	1
2	0	0	0	1	0
3	0	0	0	1	1
4	0	0	1	0	0
5	0	0	1	0	1
6	0	0	1	1	0
7	0	0	1	1	1
8	0	1	0	0	0
9	0	1	0	0	1
10	0	1	0	1	0
11	0	1	0	1	1
12	0	1	1	0	0
13	0	1	1	0	1
14	0	1	1	1	0
15	0	1	1	1	1
16	1	0	0	0	0
17	1	0	0	0	1
18	1	0	0	1	0
19	1	0	0	1	1
20	1	0	1	0	0
21	1	0	1	0	1
22	1	0	1	1	0
23	1	0	0	1	1
24	1	1	0	0	0
25	1	1	0	0	1
26	1	1	0	1	0
27	1	1	0	1	1
28	1	1	1	0	0
29	1	1	1	0	1
30	1	1	1	1	0
31	1	1	1	1	1

"You can fill this table out by looking at the patterns," I said, realizing that any onlooker who happened to poke their head in to my class would think "Oh, good, Mr. Garelick is teaching them that math is about patterns!"—a characterization that I dislike for reasons I won't get into here.

I started filling out the first four rows; once I got to the fifth row, they started to see the pattern.

"Oh, it just keeps repeating itself: 01, 10, 11, and 100," a boy said.

"What do the numbers mean?" someone else asked.

"They correspond to the numbers on the left."

"But why?"

I tried to explain, showing that you're adding powers of 2, just as in base 10 the number 11 is $(1 \times 10) + (1 \times 1)$. Some students understood, but most didn't.

I then said "Just keep filling out the table. It doesn't matter right now whether you understand what the binary numbers mean." Reaction from my imaginary onlooker who had previously liked my comment about patterns: "Oh wait; he's having them 'do' math without 'knowing' math." Or words to that effect.

Once all 31 rows were filled, I had five students transfer the numbers to five mini whiteboards. I then proceeded to do my magic trick. One student who had an interest in computers knew how it was done so he kept quiet.

The first time I revealed the number selected, the entire class shouted.

"Do it again!"

I did and was right again. Each time I revealed their number, they were now screaming.

"He's a wizard!" someone shouted.

I finally revealed the trick: "I look at the first number on each card you told me contained your number and then add them up. For example, if seven were picked, that number appears on the first three cards, but no others. The first numbers on those cards are 1, 2 and 4, which sum to seven."

There was a collective "Oh!"

I again offered the cards that I printed up and was surrounded by clamoring students, many with hands cupped as if receiving communion. While administering the mathematical sacraments, I thought about how the excitement of my algebra class with its esprit de corps stood in stark contrast to the Math 8 class who felt left behind.

I realized I had to do something to fill in the vast wasteland of the Math 8 course. And for an extra challenge, I needed to do so without the ritual of "growth mindset."

CHAPTER 6
THE PROSPECT OF A HORRIBLE PD, A HORRIBLE MEETING, AND AN UNLIKELY COLLABORATION

Many schools require teachers to attend some kind of professional development (PD), and Cypress was no exception. During my second year at Cypress, James, the other math teacher (and union representative), and I were "asked" by the superintendent to attend six all-day PD sessions over the course of the school year. The PD, held by the County Office of Education, was to be a forum for "collaboration" among math teachers in the county.

Although I don't mind collaborating with teachers, I don't like the collaboration to be prescribed with a typical educational agenda of dubious and/or ineffective practices. And certainly not for six times. I was also leery of James, who was passive-aggressively hostile. As I told Diane during one of our sessions, "I dislike the idea of going to the sessions with him more than I dislike the idea of the PD itself."

"Passive-aggressive types are the worst," she said.

As it turned out, the PD was canceled. James and I were the only two people in the county who had signed up. This might have been because it had been held the previous year with about ten math teachers (and our principal) attending. I'm guessing here that word got around that it wasn't worth attending. I'm also guessing that the superintendent had either not received the message, or our principal who thought it worthwhile convinced him that it would be good idea for us to attend.

Our delight at the cancellation was rather short-lived, however. The moderator met with our principal and suggested having a series of two-hour meetings with us at school during the early part of the day when we weren't teaching. Neither James nor I were too thrilled at the idea of collaborating with each other.

We all met one time. The moderator, a middle-aged woman who talked in the cheery tones of a facilitator, began describing how she loved math while in school but was just "following the rules and getting an answer." Later, when she taught math, she found she couldn't explain to students the underlying concepts. Which led her to say that the Common Core standards were all about "understanding," and teachers had better teach for understanding because "California's Common Core–aligned tests are not about 'answer getting' anymore!" Students had to explain their answers, and the tests evaluate whether students are able to solve problems in more than one way.

She went on almost breathlessly: "Students can get full credit on problems where they have to provide explanations—even if they get the numerical answer wrong."

James and I said nothing.

"Provided the reasoning and process are correct, of course," she added. "Explaining answers is tough for students and for this reason there is a need for discourse in the classroom and 'rich tasks.'"

My years in education school had taught me the skill of keeping my mouth shut appropriately, but at this point I couldn't contain myself and asked, "Could you define what a 'rich task' is?"

Her answer was extraordinary in its eloquence at saying absolutely nothing: "It's a problem that has multiple entry points and has various levels of cognitive demands. Every student can be successful on at least part of it."

I had had some experience with rich problems, so I knew exactly the type of problem to which she was referring; problems like "A rectangle with a perimeter of 20 inches has what dimensions?" or "How many boxes would be needed to pack and ship one million books collected in a school-based book drive?"

At this point, James spoke up. He said that meeting for two hours for six sessions was superfluous if it was just the two of us. "I teach three different math classes plus doing the IT for the school and don't have time to delve into alternative approaches other than to follow the script and curriculum as laid out in the book."

James' mention of curriculum and textbooks gave her the opening she needed. "Books are just tools," she proclaimed. "They may be strong in one area but weak in another. Traditional textbooks tend to be lacking in opportunities for conceptual understanding and are old-school in their approach."

She sensed that both of us were more than willing to let her dig her own grave here. "Though there's nothing wrong with old-school," she quickly added.

As tempting as it was. I saw no need to tell her that I used a 1962 textbook by Dolciani for my algebra class.

She asked if we relied on our textbook for a "script," meaning scope and sequence "Do you read just one textbook?" she asked me.

"I read lots of textbooks," I said.

"He's also written books," James said. I was surprised that he knew about them, but I had slipped *Math Education in the U.S.* surreptitiously in the bookcase in the teacher's lounge, so maybe he had read it.

"How nice!" she said and feigned an interest by asking what they were about. I gave a "rich" answer.

"Math education," I said.

"Wonderful!"

Since James had played up my authorship, I decided to return the favor.

"Neither of us teaches in a vacuum," I said. "I read lots of textbooks and talk to lots of teachers. And James has a lot more experience than I do so he isn't exactly ignorant about how to teach math. I really don't think that this two-hour collaboration is going to add much more."

I realized this opened me up to her protesting that perhaps I could benefit from his experience so I needed to head that off. "Besides, I'm getting mixed messages," I said. "On the one hand, I'm told by the administration that I'm doing great, and I hear from parents that I'm doing great. But then I'm told that I *must* attend this PD. Is there something about my teaching that's lacking? What is this about?"

She assured us that there's nothing lacking in our teaching and that she's sure we are both fantastic teachers. "What is it then? Is this about test scores? They think this will raise test scores?"

She had no answer for this except something that I can't remember. She saw the handwriting on the wall and said, "No use beating a dead horse," and then she said she would talk to the administration about it. And that was the end of our PD.

I decided that the next time I met with Diane, I would tell her about the success of James's and my "collaboration."

Chapter 7

A CATHARTIC DISCUSSION,
PUTTING THE BELL ON THE CAT,
AND BUSINESS AS USUAL

In my meetings with Diane we sometimes discussed my interactions with other teachers, which I found fairly enjoyable. Even though it's not quite gossip, it does have cathartic benefits.

I told Diane about the meeting James and I had the week before where we avoided the PD sessions on how best to teach math. Diane asked, "Are you getting along with James any better?"

"Well, he was definitely friendlier toward me after that meeting."

"So there's been a breakthrough," Diane said.

"I wouldn't go that far," I said. "He was friendly for a few days. He's back in his non-talkative passive-aggressive mode."

"I've met his wife," Diane disclosed. "She works as a counselor at a high school near here. She's very nice," she said and sipped her coffee while looking at me out of the sides of her eyes. "Except when she isn't," she added.

"Sounds like a marriage made in heaven," I said.

"I find when I talk to teachers that one of the biggest complaints about teaching is not always the teaching itself. It's frequently about getting along with other teachers," she said.

This made a lot of sense. One event in particular came to mind. During my first year at Cypress, the superintendent was pushing for having seven periods rather than six. This meant that our classes would be forty-five minutes long instead of fifty-five. It would be even shorter on Wednesdays when we were dismissed early because of the weekly staff meeting.

The seven-period day, in fact, was the topic of discussion at one such staff meeting, led by the superintendent. Prior to the meeting, two of the teachers were in the room and they agreed with me that shorter class times were not a good idea.

"You're right," one of the teachers said. "It would really end up forcing us to cram a lot of things in." She said she would speak out against it.

When our meeting began, the superintendent talked up the benefits of the new schedule because it would allow students to now have two electives instead of just limiting them to one. And an elective could also be two periods long: sixth and seventh periods. With more electives, this could open up more teaching opportunities—an important consideration given that the largest class was graduating and enrollment numbers were dwindling.

"But I want to hear from all of you," he said. "What are your feelings about this schedule?"

The silence that followed reminded me of Aesop's fable about which mouse was going to put the bell on the cat.

Given the discussion prior to the meeting, I felt I was on safe ground to start the discussion.

"I'm not for it," I said.

All eyes were suddenly on me.

"A shorter class period will make it difficult to teach. Right now, Wednesdays are my worst days because class length is 45 minutes and I often don't get done what needs to be done. With seven periods, every day will be like Wednesdays are now—and Wednesdays will be even shorter."

"So I take it that you would be voting 'no' on this?"

I wasn't aware that this was a vote, but now so informed I replied, "That would be safe to say."

Discussion continued. The Drama and PE teachers concurred with me, and then it was James's turn.

"I think this would be a good step forward," he said. "I would like the opportunity to reinvent myself as a teacher…" and other words to that effect.

After he spoke, others now seemed to approve of the seven-period day, including the teacher who had previously agreed with me earlier that it was a bad idea.

"I can't blame her," I told Diane. "She's worried about her job and didn't want to be against the superintendent. Plus I think James being the union rep kind of makes him the thought leader."

"Don't get me started on teachers' unions," she said. "I'm starting to get a whole different take on this now."

The union influence, such as it was, didn't hold a candle to the history teacher's final words on the subject. He had taught at the school for 30 years and was well respected. Although he voted in favor of the seven-period day he offered this reflection after the yeas were seen to outweigh the nays: "I think it's a shame that we'll be going into the next school year with some people not happy about this change and a cloud hanging over them. So I propose we think about this some more."

Evidently, the superintendent did. At the next staff meeting, he announced that the current six-period schedule would remain, although he was disappointed in the reaction. I guess he wanted unanimity. Apparently, James was disgruntled about it as well.

"I don't know if he's held it against me," I told Diane.

"He might have," she said. "It's hard to say."

It's hard to say a lot of things that go on in any school. I recall another time—this one at a party. James was talking with the third-grade teacher who mentioned the downward trend of state test scores in math at Cypress School.

James gave her a reason for that. "It's because we don't have students collaborate with each other enough," he told her. She nodded in agreement at what is accepted as educational wisdom. Given his resistance to the PD we avoided about teacher collaboration I've found his "not enough collaboration" stance ironic.

I decided to not bring up the overheard party conversation at this session with Diane. Despite her dislike of unions and distrust of people who represent them, she was likely to say, "Well he does bring up a good point about student collaboration; what are your thoughts?" There were plenty of other avenues open to her to explore my thoughts on dubious and/or ineffective educational practices. No need to give her ideas.

Chapter 8
NOT MAKING SENSE, AND A CONVERSATION
I NEVER HAD

"Math doesn't make sense." This was the chief complaint that Lucy evinced when seeking help with algebra. She was a bright girl in my eighth-grade algebra class at St. Stephens.

Lucy's statement will no doubt serve as evidence for those who view me as an unbending traditionalist hell-bent on teaching procedures at the expense of understanding. Although I do provide the concepts that underly various procedures, there are students, like Lucy, for whom math had always come easy and the connection between procedure and concept was obvious. With algebra, the level of abstraction ramps up and things become more complex. Lucy thought that if math didn't come easy, then either something was wrong with her, or math made no sense.

The range of abilities in the St. Stephens algebra class was much wider than in my previous classes and likely more typical of most schools. There were about five students at St. Stephens who were at the very top of the class. At the lower end, there were about four or five. Lucy was starting to fall into that lower group. She made a good effort in my algebra class in the beginning but increasingly got caught in waves of confusion starting with multiplying and dividing powers.

She had begun to make a good comeback with factoring of trinomials such as x^2+5x+6 into two binomials: $(x+2)(x+3)$. She even volunteered to do a problem at the board. But the next day, we had more complex trinomials like $6x^2-5x-6$. Students were having a hard time with these and Lucy was back to sitting with arms folded, answering questions I asked of her with a shrug and a response of "I don't know" laden with teenaged insouciance.

I had taught this particular type of trinomial by using a trial-and-error method in which you try various factors like $2x$ and $3x$, and $6x$ and x to get it to work. (If you're curious, the factorization of $6x^2-5x-6$ is $(2x-3)(3x+2)$.)

There is another method, sometimes called the "diamond method," which involves some steps that I won't go into here, but which results in the trinomial being expressed as $6x^2-9x+4x-6$. This can then be written as $3x(2x-3) + 2(2x-3)$. Because $(2x-3)$ is a common factor, this now can be expressed as $(2x-3)$ $(3x+2)$. I've tried to teach this method in the past with mixed success; many find it difficult. Given the problems I was having with Lucy and others, I decided to stick with the trial-and-error method.

I allotted time in every class for students to start on their homework to allow me to offer help and guidance. She accepted my help grudgingly. After working through a problem, I asked, "Does it make sense now?"

She gave her usual response. "Sort of."

Katherine would sometimes use that period to catch up on paperwork and in so doing would observe what was going on in class. She never offered any criticism or comments on anything that happened unless I asked. (And when you get down to it, that's how I like to be mentored.) When I saw Katherine later that day, I told her, "I'm at my wits end with Lucy."

"I know," she said. "One look at her body language tells you she's given up."

"I've tried everything," I said. "I've communicated with her mother, let her know she can get help, but she doesn't even try. I feel like saying 'I'm bending over backward for you; the least you can do is show some respect and make an effort.'"

"You should tell her that," she said. "Just talk with her and tell her what you told me, and what your expectations are. She'll be real honest with you, but you need to reach an understanding."

I lost sleep that night rehearsing how that conversation would go. I decided I would pull her aside when the rest of the class was doing their warm-up questions and have the talk. But when I arrived in the classroom, I was greeted by a very cheerful Lucy who offered to help me pass out the day's warm-up questions to the class. She then excitedly told me, "I found a way to do the factoring."

She showed me. It was the diamond method I had decided not to teach because I thought it would be too confusing for her.

"Where did you learn this?" I asked.

"I looked it up on the internet. It's really easy."

"Fantastic," I said. "Do you want to show the class how it's done?"

She didn't want to, so I demonstrated the method. There were the sounds of people getting it as I put some problems on the board for them to work. I left the class elated that Lucy had taken the initiative and was getting it.

I ran into Katherine after class was over and excitedly told her about Lucy's miraculous turnaround. As it turned out, after Katherine had talked with me the previous day, she decided to talk with Lucy at the end of the day.

"That explains her change in attitude," I said.

"I should have told you," she said. "I'm sorry. But she was in the classroom getting something so I just talked to her."

"What did you tell her?"

"I told her that her body language is telling us she's given up."

"Anything else?"

"I said, 'Mr. Garelick thinks you don't like him.'"

I wished she hadn't said that. "What did she say to that?" I asked.

"She said, 'Oh no, that's not true.' She felt bad."

That evening, my wife, who was brought up Catholic, said this was part of Catholic guilt. I have chosen to remain agnostic on such matters.

In the end, the top students were able to work the diamond method, while the other students relied on the trial-and-error method. Lucy would forget the procedure she had found on the internet, and even simple trinomials would elude her despite the fact that factoring trinomials doesn't go away in subsequent lessons.

There is an advantage to continued practice should anyone have their doubts. It leads to proficiency and eventually can connect with the understanding and "sense" that Lucy felt was lacking.

She would continue to be a challenge. And I would learn to take my victories if and when they occurred.

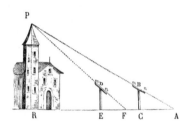

CHAPTER 9
A GNARLY PROBLEM, CRITICAL THINKING, AND AUTHENTIC STRUGGLE

My meetings with my parole office/mentor Diane occurred once a week in the early morning at a local coffee house a few blocks from the Cypress School. At one particular meeting, she showed me her notes from an observation she had made of a lesson I gave my seventh-grade class. Her notes were typical "hunting for problems" comments, such as my not noticing a particular boy who was unfocused, or another student who was talking, and so on.

"Any comments?" she asked.

I resisted the urge to say that it sounded like she was looking for problems to enter on her online checklist. I talked instead about the lesson itself. It had been about taking a situation like "A bowling alley charges $5 for shoes and $3 per game bowled" and writing an algebraic expression for the cost of x games. (5 + 3x). Knowing that Diane wanted to see me extend JUMP's scaffolded approach to more "gnarly" problems, I told her about a problem I gave the seventh graders on one of the warm-up questions the day after the lesson she observed.

They were to write an expression representing the cost for n hours if a babysitter charges a flat fee of $10 and $15 per hour but with the first hour free. I was met with the usual question of "How do you do this?"

In my highly scientific approach, I helped the first person who asked "How do you do this?" which happened to be Kyle. He was a talkative boy who was quite good at problems when he put his mind to it.

"How many hours does the babysitter charge for 6 hours of work if the first hour is free?" I asked.

"Five," he answered.

"Right. 6 – 1 = 5. So what does he charge for five hours of work?"

"Five minus one," he said. I gave him a few more numbers and then asked, "How much for n hours of work?"

"Oh! $n - 1$," he said. He then saw that it was $10 + 15(n - 1)$, although he and others needed help with the parentheses.

"Yes, that's a good problem," Diane said. "But it wasn't really critical thinking."

"Why not?" I asked.

"You led them there."

I said nothing, hoping for an awkward silence and getting my wish.

"There's nothing wrong with what you did," she said. "But true critical thinking would involve them struggling to come up with a solution."

I recognized this immediately as the "struggle is good" philosophy, which holds that if students aren't struggling, they aren't learning. There are nuances to this philosophy, including "productive struggle," "desirable difficulties," and "students should be able to use prior knowledge in new situations without scaffolding because otherwise it is inauthentic." I've read variations of this thinking in books that I've thrown across the room.

"Let me give you a problem that I want you to solve," I said. "Two cars head toward each other on the same highway. One car starts from the north heading south, at 80 mph. The other car starts from the south heading north at 70 mph. They meet somewhere on the highway. How far apart are they 1 hour before they meet?"

She took a gulp of coffee and tried to smile.

"You do not need to know the distance they are apart to solve it," I said.

She looked perplexed and gave me the same look I see on my students' faces when they ask "How do you do this?"

"Tell me this," I said. "How far does a car going 80 mph travel in 1 hour?"

"Eighty miles," she said.

I drew a line on a napkin and marked a point near the middle with an *X*. "Where was the 80 mph car 1 hour before he got here?"

"Well, that would be 80 miles north of that point."

"What about the 70 mph car?"

"Uh, 70 miles south of the point?"

"Good. Can you put that together somehow?"

She suddenly saw it. "Oh, I see! They're 150 miles apart 1 hour before they meet."

"Good work. Now, let me ask you something. I gave you some hints. Would you say that you used those hints in thinking about the problem and coming up with a solution?"

She smiled knowingly. "Ah, I see. Critical thinking."

"So, would you say that what you did qualifies as critical thinking?" She agreed.

"Then why would you say that what I did with the babysitting question did not qualify as critical thinking."

"I'll have to think about what I mean by critical thinking," she said. "I think applying an algorithm repeatedly does not entail critical thinking."

"Even if it leads to a conclusion? And in essence that was what I had you do when you think about it. And you put it together like my students did. Why would you not call that critical thinking? In your mind, is there no difference between thinking and critical thinking?"

"I guess I might have to look up the definition of critical thinking."

"I'll send you a definition tonight by email," I said. "My concern is this. If your goal is to look for examples of critical thinking in my classes using the definition you've presented, you will probably never see critical thinking in my classes. I use worked examples and scaffolding and problems that ramp up. That's how I teach. You'll see this more in my algebra class, and I hope you'll observe one of those."

She said she definitely would. I thanked her for having the discussion with me. "I felt it was important that we understand the language we're speaking and what I'm about."

"Yes," she said. The conversation then shifted to lighter topics. I felt a bit bad for putting her on the spot with my math problem. But then again, her struggle with critical thinking was productive if not authentic.

CHAPTER 10
MORE ON MAKING SENSE, AND A
FICKLE BOOKSELLER

What *making sense* means varies for different people. For Lucy, if she could do the procedure, it made sense. Same for most of the seventh graders I've taught, although there are other "nuances" depending on the person and at what level of silliness or seriousness they were operating.

My Math 7 class at St. Stephens was a mix of different abilities and personalities. John was an aspiring athlete who had difficulty with math facts and remembering procedures. He worked earnestly and trusted me, but felt that ultimately math wasn't something he would need. His vision of the future was that he would be a superstar in the sports world and have enough money to hire people to do various chores—math being one of the things.

Whereas Lucy from my algebra class might utter "That doesn't make sense," John was more likely to say "That's a lot of work" when faced with tedious procedures like adding or subtracting large mixed numbers.

He once asked in all seriousness why I assigned so many problems. I asked if there was a particular play in baseball that he had to practice a lot. There was—it was a tricky play that first basemen had to perform automatically and perfectly. "It's the same thing in math," I said. "We have to practice certain procedures so we can use them automatically to solve problems."

Two-second pause; then: "But Mr. G., I *like* baseball."

My reply was performed automatically and perfectly. "You don't have to like math; you just have to know how to do it."

Donna, another student in that same class, had a different idea of sense, which vacillated between childish whimsy and pubescent whimsy.

Example of childish whimsy: After I explained that letters representing numbers were numbers going by different names, she proclaimed that the number 10 should be called "Jerry."

Example of pubescent whimsy: I had passed out a worksheet that had on it a problem asking for the area of the shaded portion of the figure below:

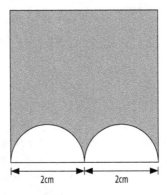

Upon seeing the figure, Donna shouted, "What the ?!" and covered her mouth to stifle a giggle. When I came over to see what was the matter she turned the paper over so the figure would be out of sight. She did not disclose the source of her outburst to anyone in her class, but started to work on the problems.

Looking at the picture a few minutes later, I could see that one could interpret it to be any of two portions of human anatomy, one of which lacked nipples.

A completely different facet of the word *sense* came from my seventh grade student Jimmy the year before at the Cypress School. I have previously described his penchant for asking questions during a lesson on multiplication of negative numbers. Before I could teach multiplication of negative numbers, however, JUMP Math required covering how to evaluate expressions such as $3 - (2 - x)$.

Knowing how to multiply by negative numbers would make this a lot easier. But JUMP decided on a micro-scaffolded approach, which in retrospect I would not choose to do again. JUMP's approach was to first look at something with no variables like $10 - (5 - 2)$.

"We know we can do this easily by just doing the subtraction in the parentheses first," I said. "So we get $10 - 3$ which is 7. But suppose I wanted to do it by distribution."

"Why would we want to do that when we can just subtract what's in the parentheses?" Jimmy asked.

"Because pretty soon we're going to evaluate expressions like $3 - (2 - x)$ where we don't know the value inside the parentheses."

This quieted him for the moment, so I went on. I decided to make up a story to go along with the problem. "Say you visit a bookseller and he says to Jimmy, 'I'm going to give you a special deal. I'm going to reduce the price of this $10 book by $5.'"

"Yeah, that would be a good deal," Jimmy said.

"Yes, it is, but then at the last minute he says, 'I changed my mind. I'm only going to take off $3.'"

"Wait a minute, he said he was going to take off $5," Jimmy said.

"Right. So you're going to pay more, aren't you? Originally you would have paid $10 - 5$, which is $5. But he reduced the discount by $2. So how much more are you going to pay now?"

Jimmy thought a minute. "Two dollars more."

"Right," I said. "If I wrote it now as $10 - (5 - 2)$, we can see that you end up paying two more dollars than what you would have paid had he not changed his mind. And what you end up paying can be written as $10 - 5 + 2$."

The whole idea being that we evaluated the expression using an intuitive approach, thereby sidestepping multiplication of each number by – 1. As I say, I wasn't fond of the approach. Jimmy was strangely silent.

"Now, let's suppose at the last minute the bookseller says, 'Wait, I changed my mind; I'm going to take off $7.' Now you're paying less than you would have if he only took off $5. How much less?"

"Two dollars," Jimmy said with a sigh.

I then summarized it as a rule: The signs of the numbers inside become the opposite. The homework problems were to evaluate various expressions in this manner, including those with variables, like $10 - (5 - x)$.

"It just doesn't make sense," Jimmy said.

"What doesn't?" I asked.

"I don't understand why he would give less of a discount than he said he would. The guy said he would take $5 off, and then he only takes $3 off. Why would he do this? What sense does that make?"

"The bookseller is a bit strange, I admit," I said. "But on the other hand, in the end he took off $2 more than he said he would. So he's not all bad."

"I don't trust him," he said. "I wouldn't come back to his store."

With Jimmy it was hard to tell whether his questioning was serious or a means of wasting time. Either possibility made sense.

Chapter 11

THE GENERAL THIS 'N THAT SHOP,
NEGATIVE NUMBERS, AND FAITH

I went to school at University of Michigan in the late 1960s/early 1970s, long before the proliferation of 24-hour 7-Eleven stores, Starbucks, and other brand-name franchises. A few blocks away from me was a small mom-and-pop grocery store that was fairly new called "The General This 'n That Shop." During one particularly cold winter, I noticed that the items in the store were dwindling and it seemed that they weren't going to be around for too much longer. One day, I stopped by to find that most of the shelves were bare, and on one, a single loaf of bread remained, which I bought.

"Are you going out of business?" I asked the cashier.

Her response: "I hope not."

It is this type of optimism that I try to instill in my students. And among my seventh-grade students, the topic of negative numbers has served as the first building block of success that leads to it.

I do not like to prolong the topic. I once observed a teacher taking three weeks to teach it. The students had it down fairly well when the teacher introduced a new explanation using colored circles, causing confusion. One girl asked, "Why are we doing this?"

The teacher answered, "I know you know how to add and subtract with negative numbers. Now I want you to understand why it works."

The girl's response: "I don't want to understand!"

This incident is not unique. I've found that a lot of the confusion with the addition and subtraction of negative integers comes from giving students more techniques and pictorials than are really needed. They are left with the impression that it is a complex process and that there are many different ways to do it.

I keep it relatively straightforward with the first day spent using number lines with arrows to compute addition of negative numbers. The next day, the addition is done without pictures.

I then introduce subtraction. I tried this with an accelerated seventh-grade class during my first year teaching at Cypress School. I asked them to compute $6 + (-4)$, which they knew how to do from the previous lesson. Two was their answer. I then asked them to compute $6 - 4$. They saw the connection almost immediately, leading to the general rule of "adding the opposite."

While it worked well with my accelerated class, I thought maybe I wouldn't have the same success the next year with the seventh-grade class that had large deficits in their math knowledge. But the technique worked just fine, with Kyle shouting out: "Adding a negative number is the same thing as subtraction." This became a quote that I posted on the quote wall.

The only rub in all this is the subtraction of a negative number. I used to introduce this by first asking if anyone could solve $10 - (-5)$, and then linking the question to football for those who liked or played it: "After a loss of 5 yards, how many yards do you need to get a first down?" As I mentioned in an earlier chapter, Jimmy had answered, "Can't you just punt it?" I have since changed my tactics. I specify that the ball has to be run and then use any number of non-football examples such as: "It was -10 degrees yesterday and 20 degrees today.

56

By how much did it increase?"

My goal in teaching adding and subtracting of negative numbers is to achieve a level of automaticity so that students can ultimately solve a problem like 3 – 7 without using pictures or writing it as 3 + (–7). At the same time, I try to get them to develop a number sense as to whether their answer is going to be negative or positive. I give them models to use, such as: "If I gain 3 yards and lose 7, am I ahead or behind and by how much? If I earn $3 but owe $7, am I ahead or "in the hole" and by how much? They do get it, although they need reminders through the year.

And as far as multiplying negative numbers, I provide an illustration of why things work as they do. I use an example of making a video of someone riding a bike backward, and running the video backward.

"What if they were skateboarding?" Jimmy asked.

"Whatever you want," I said.

If the backward rate is represented as -3 mph and we run the video backward at 2 times the normal speed—represented as –2—the person appears to be riding a bike or skateboarding forward at 6 mph. A similar model can be used to show why a negative number times a positive is a negative number. (For the more curious students, and certainly in accelerated classes and in eighth-grade algebra, I show the proof using the distributive rule.)

Although my backward video example generally does the job, it didn't with Jimmy even when I used skateboarding rather than a bicycle. He tended to be quite literal. "That's in a video; does it work in real life?" he asked, thus opening up the question of whether mathematics can apply to images.

He finally accepted the example used in JUMP Math where someone on a mountain is descending at a rate of 30 feet per minute or –30 ft/min. The example asks how one would represent where the mountain climber had been relative to his present position 3 minutes earlier, or –3 min. Jimmy agreed that the person would be higher 3 minutes previous and further accepted that the situation is represented by –3 ×–30, or +90.

Although Jimmy understood it, a girl said she did not understand either example.

"For now, just work with the rule," I said. "You'll get it the more you work with these kind of problems." The girl did understand the examples a few days later.

"Sometimes you just have to have faith in the math," I told her. She evinced no expression so I said nothing more. Which is a good thing because I doubt she really wanted to hear about how we're all sometimes like the cashier at the General This 'n That Shop.

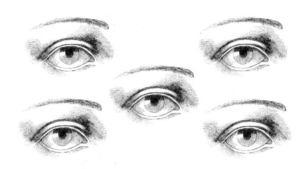

CHAPTER 12
A CLASSROOM OBSERVATION, AN EVALUATION, AND SENSE-MAKING AGAIN

The nice thing about being observed by someone in administration is that the students are well behaved for fear of being punished. Students are receptive, answer questions, and cooperate. Such was the case at Cyprus School during my second year there. The superintendent informed me that he would be observing my seventh-grade class. The lesson that day was straightforward: multiplying decimals. I didn't have them work in groups or make posters at the back of the room as I had done for Diane. I thought I'd see if that affected my evaluation—I live an exciting life.

A week later I met with the superintendent in his office to go over the results. He handed me his filled-out form, had me read it, and asked if I had any questions.

The evaluation was all very positive, going beyond what was observed in the classroom and ending with the following: "Mr. Garelick has done a good job of being a professional who takes care of business without stirring up unnecessary controversy or conflict." Which told me he hadn't read any of my articles or books on math education.

"So, do you want to come back next year?" he asked.

"I think so," I said.

"Well, I hope you will; you've been doing great. The students like you; I hear good reports from the parents. You teach well. And I can get things going to make you permanent," he said.

"I thought I couldn't be permanent unless I was full-time," I said. I taught two classes and a remediation session.

"No, you don't have to be full-time. We can make you permanent."

"Would I be teaching the same classes next year that I'm teaching now?"

He pointed to a schedule he had on the wall, showing that my classes would be the same.

"Yes, I'd like to do that," I said.

"Let's do it."

The next day I ran into James in the copy room and, feeling in a somewhat confident mood, said "I had my evaluation yesterday and found out we'll both be teaching the same classes we're teaching this year. So since you'll be teaching Math 8 again, I'll be writing up my observations of my seventh graders so you know how best to work with them."

"This is the first I've heard about that," he said. Talking with James at times was like walking in a mine field; you never knew what was going to tick him off.

"Well, he showed me the schedule."

"He hasn't talked to me about it," he said.

"OK, fine," I said and acted like I suddenly remembered something that I had to do, and left.

About two weeks later, the superintendent called me in to his office.

"I hate to tell you this," he started, "but I need to because it will come up at the next school board meeting, and I didn't want you to hear it from someone else."

Call me a pessimist but I knew that this couldn't possibly be good news.

"We're going to have to let you go, and I want you to know it has nothing to do with performance. You're doing great as I told you, but the way schools work, last one hired is the first one to go in situations like this."

I asked the most logical question I could think of: "What is the situation?"

"I'm not at liberty to say. But under contract rules I have to give you this notice prior to mid-March. It could be rescinded if things change, but I have to issue this notice now."

"I don't know what to say," I said.

"I'm sorry," he said and that ended the meeting. He did not look happy.

A week or so later, after the school board met, the superintendent gave me a copy of the board's vote to eliminate a position; four to one in favor of elimination. The document included the rationale: because of declining enrollment, the number of students would fall below a certain level. By law, the number of permanent positions had to be reduced. And—as the superintendent had told me—last one hired is first one fired.

He had me sign it and said I could request a hearing if I wanted to appeal it, but he advised against it. "The chances of convincing the board to reverse the decision is pretty small," he said.

At my weekly meeting with Diane, I told her the news. "I'm sorry to hear that," she said. "But when I was a principal, I had to sign a lot of those notices, and they were rescinded in the fall. So there may be a chance."

"It doesn't look like it, what with declining enrollments," I said.

"Well, you never know. But it sure doesn't help to have that happen. Have you told anyone?"

"No," I said. "I don't want to make an issue of it, and I certainly don't want the students to know."

"Good decision," she said. "Very professional."

"I have a question, though. I don't know too much about teachers unions and all that."

"Consider yourself lucky," she said.

"Well, here's my question. Shouldn't the union rep have been there at the meeting when the superintendent told me the news?"

"He wasn't? You didn't tell me that."

"No," I said.

"That doesn't make sense."

"You're starting to sound like my students," I said.

"Has James talked to you about it at all?"

"He's continuing to not give me the time of day."

"Are you planning on talking to him?"

"No," I said. "It doesn't sound like there's anything he can do. And even if he could, something tells me he wouldn't."

"Hard to say," she said. "Well, maybe not that hard. I hope it gets rescinded."

I told none of the teachers nor the students and went on as normal. Normal for me is like the proverbial actor before curtain, suddenly struck with panic that he has forgotten all his lines and even what the play is about. But once the students come into the room, it's "curtain up": the play is on. School politics and its various nuances are not part of it.

Chapter 13
FAULTY ASSUMPTIONS, THE BEST OF INTENTIONS, AND A CROAKING FROG

In planning my future classes during the summer before the upcoming school year, I proceed from an undying faith in my expectations. During the actual school year, I then deal with the reality. In the end, it is always astounding to me how some intuitions turn out surprisingly well.

My Math 7 class at Cypress my second year was the non-accelerated version. I had taught accelerated Math 7 the year before, but I was now faced with a challenging group of students whom I knew were disheartened about math and likely dreading the upcoming year. While planning my lessons during the summer using the JUMP Math teacher's manual, I had a vision that the students would, upon succeeding and getting good grades on tests and quizzes, eventually discover that the math was actually interesting and that they could manage it.

The reality was slightly different, as I found out. I knew that *something* was happening. Just not in the manner I had imagined.

The next year when I started at St. Stephens, I found that my Math 8 class was similar in some respects to the Math 7 class. I had assumed during my planning that the ability level would be high, thinking that was the norm for private schools. I therefore sought to overcome the vast wasteland of disparate topics and dearth of algebra that is typical for Math 8 by introducing more algebra than is usually included, drawing upon the simpler problems and approach in another book authored by Dolciani called *Basic Algebra*.

I selected some topics that I thought would provide a basic grounding in algebraic concepts that would help them when they took the regular Algebra 1 class in ninth grade. These topics included multiplying polynomials, factoring, algebraic fractions, and various word problems.

As it turned out, my Math 8 class was at a different ability level than I had pictured during the summer. I was starting to have doubts about my plan to squeeze in basic algebra for the Math 8 class despite my having worked out lesson plans for the same. In addition to the disparate set of topics that make up Math 8, the class had become a disparate set of students. The two girls with whom I had been doing intervention work were on a separate track. I would work with them two days per week during their first period, bringing them up to speed on very elementary equations, percents, decimals, and fractions—and insisting they learn their multiplication facts.

Despite the doubts I had for squeezing in more algebra, I realized one day that I would have to go through with it. My revelation came after a bout of rainstorms that left puddles throughout the campus and a tree frog next to my Batcave classroom. I don't know for sure that it was a tree frog, but it was definitely a frog—and it croaked. Its croak was distinctive and almost as loud as the crows that occasionally rested in the palm tree outside.

One day, as the class was starting to work on the homework I had assigned, the croak of the tree frog filled the room. This provided a distraction that the eight students wasted no time acting on.

"Can we look for the frog?" they asked. "Jared is really good at catching them." Jared had an albino snake at home and was known for being proficient at catching lizards, which also populated the school campus at times.

These days, one hears that all teaching must be done with "intentionality." This is the current edu-buzzword that has replaced the previous one: "student agency." From what I can tell, *intentionality* generally means an overriding goal that strongly colors—and drags along—all other considerations of a lesson. I decided that if anyone asked about my intentions, I would say that looking for an elusive frog was what I intended to happen.

"Let's do it!" I said, and the class ran out, looking for the croaking frog. Jared scaled up a hill on the other side of the narrow outside corridor that led to the classroom. They looked in vain for a frog that croaked when least expected and somehow made it sound like it was coming from the narrow corridor—where it was not. Most of the time, however, it knew when to keep its mouth shut.

During the futile five-minute search for the frog, I decided that I had no choice but to go ahead with my original plan—or should I say intentions—to teach the basic algebra.

My reasoning had more to do with the remaining months of school than anything else. The textbook the school used for Math 8 was one of those that had one day devoted to a "discovery"-type activity and the next day a "direct instruction"-type lesson. Book publishers tout this as a balanced approach, usually on their front covers. I tend to skip the discovery-type lessons and teach the traditional-style lessons, supplementing heavily from older textbooks. This left me with little remaining of the book and a lot of time to fill until end of school.

The next day, I announced my plan to the class. "We will be learning some more algebra," I said. "In fact, it is the same algebra you will learn when you take algebra next year." They became strangely quiet.

"This will have an advantage," I continued. "When you take algebra next year, many of the concepts and procedures will be familiar."

Silence.

"Any questions?"

The croak of the tree frog then filled the room.

"It's back," I said. I decided in that moment to ease up on explaining my intentions about "Let's try this one more time."

We went outside, Jared scaled the hill again, others looked in the narrow corridor—all to no avail. We went back to the room, and I got them started on a lesson about factoring. As they worked the problems, I felt deep down that the tree frog's croak was intentional and my decision was all part of his plan.

Chapter 14

OPERATING AXIOMS, THE DEATH MARCH
TO THE QUADRATIC FORMULA, AND AN
UNIMPRESSED STUDENT TEACHER

In math, assumptions held to be self-evident are accepted without proof and are called *axioms*. In teaching, as in many situations in life, one also makes many assumptions. I accept them without proof not because they are self-evident but because 1) they seem like they *could* be true and 2) I lack absolute proof. My axioms change from day to day depending on circumstance and observation, but eventually they coalesce into a consistent set. Associated theorems then follow with the proviso that I could be dead wrong.

During my first year at Cypress I was forming many axioms, particularly for my algebra class. It was a small class—only 11 students—and included two sets of twin girls. One set determined the tone of the class—they were somewhat dour and projected a "don't mess with me" vibe. The other twins were very bright, and students clamored to be seated next to or near them whenever I changed the seating.

The class was unusually quiet and for the first few months I was always in doubt as to where I stood with them. It wasn't until about March when we hit the chapter on quadratic equations that I felt I was hitting my stride and getting to know them.

At the start of the chapter I announced that we would now be continuing on our death march to the quadratic formula. "We've learned to solve some types of quadratic equations by factoring, but now we're going to look at more complicated cases when we can't factor," I said. "By Friday of this week, we will learn the quadratic formula." I then wrote it on the board:

$$X = \frac{-b \pm \sqrt{b^2 - 4ac}}{2a}$$

I tend to stay away from things like posting "Today's Objective" because most students ignore them—as do I. I find it far more effective to let them know what they'll be doing in a week's time or even a month's. Case in point: The looks of horror and disbelief on their faces as they viewed the formula told me I had their attention. "By Friday, this will not look as ominous to you as it does now," I said.

And sure enough, by the time Friday came, and after working with solving quadratic equations by completing the square, they were ready for the much easier way of solving equations by the formula. After they felt comfortable with it, I told them that next week I would show them how the formula is derived.

"What does deriving the formula mean?" one of the dour twins asked.

"It means solving the equation $ax^2 + bx + c = 0$ using the steps of completing the square."

Silence.

"And the derivation of the quadratic formula will be an extra credit problem worth 10 points."

"It must be hard," the other dour twin said.

"I don't think it's hard," I said. "If you can complete the square, you can derive the formula."

"I love completing the square," one of the bright twins said.

Earlier that week, the third-grade teacher, Sandra, had asked me if the student teacher she was mentoring in her class could observe one of my lessons. "She's interested in teaching middle school math and wants to see a class."

"She doesn't want to teach elementary school?" I asked.

"She's exploring options."

"Does she know what middle school is like?"

"I think that's why she wants to observe a class," Sandra said. Sandra had in fact taught algebra at Cypress a few years before, team teaching with James, the union representative. An opening for a third-grade teacher came up and Sandra went for it, apparently preferring it to middle school.

"Fine," I said. "I'm deriving the quadratic formula next Monday in my algebra class. Have her come by."

The student teacher was in her twenties and projected an aura of confidence that comes from a belief that the (forgive me) crap ideas she had been fed in ed school were actually worth following. (I feel fairly confident in assuming this as an axiom.)

I started my lesson that day by pointing to a poster I had made which bore a quote from Rene Descartes: "Each problem that I solved became a rule which served afterwards to solve other problems."

"Nowhere is this more evident in Algebra 1 than in the derivation of the quadratic formula," I said, and proceeded to show the steps. The students knew how to complete the square, having done it as part of last week's death march. As I worked through the derivation, I asked them for next steps. For the most part, they knew them, although it often took some prodding. I note that this is how I normally teach but I was particularly aware of keeping up a dialogue lest I be judged guilty of too much "teacher talk"—one of the criticisms levied against traditional teaching.

At the end of the class, the student teacher left without a thank you—or anything. Her head was held obnoxiously high. I assume but cannot prove that she thought that all I was doing was promoting memorization and imitation of procedures, but not "deeper understanding."

I never heard from Sandra on what the student teacher might have thought. And in fact, I noticed that Sandra was no longer as friendly to me as she once had been. I assume (and again cannot prove) that I was somehow discredited in her eyes.

I did ask Sandra how her student teacher was doing, hoping to get some feedback. "Oh, she's doing some innovative things in the classroom," she said. What these innovative things were she didn't say, nor did I ask. I believe with some degree of confidence that it involved group work; collaboration; student-centered, inquiry-based projects; and not answering students' questions.

As it stands, four out of my eleven students got the derivation correct on the test. Two or three more got partial credit for getting halfway through. I hold out belief that at least one person was as fascinated as I was years ago in seeing how a method for solving problems could be turned into a formula. I have no proof of this of course.

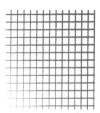

CHAPTER 15
PROFESSIONAL DEVELOPMENT, MEMORIZATION, AND DUBIOUS RUBRICS

As part of the parole/credentialing process, I was required to have nine hours of

professional development (PD) for the school year. I didn't realize it at the time, but a conference I attended prior to my starting at Cypress came in handy when it came time for my first mentor, Ellen, to fill in the electronic checklist on PD.

I had attended a conference given at Oxford University, sponsored by a grass-roots organization called researchED, a teacher-led organization dedicated to disseminating information on effective teaching practices backed by scientific research. I had, in fact, given a presentation at this conference about the state of math education in the U.S., how it got that way, and how it looked like it was going to stay there thanks to Common Core.

I asked Ellen whether I could count my attendance at the researchED conference, given that it occurred in the summer before I started at Cypress. "Of course it does," she said. "I wish we could count it double, since you presented there."

She didn't ask what my presentation was about, nor did I volunteer it. In fact no one at the school ever asked. Although I'd like to paint myself as a totally altruistic hero, I have to say I really wish someone had shown even the slightest interest.

"Can you describe a session that you attended?" Ellen asked.

I told her about a session on the role of memory in learning and understanding. She looked at me over her laptop.

"Memorization?" she asked.

"Yes."

"Memorization is not a good thing," she said as if she were talking about parents beating their children. "Was this person advocating it?"

"It was about how memory plays a role in learning."

"How?"

This wasn't looking good. "You taught biology, right? Did you need to know a lot of information?"

"Well, yes."

"Names of organisms, what's in a cell, and things of that nature? Somehow that gets into your long-term memory, doesn't it?"

She started typing information into her electronic form. "Okay, how does this sound?" she asked. "The session focused on long-term memory and its role in understanding."

"Sounds good," I said. She did not appear entirely convinced that this was true, but she did look satisfied that it would pass muster by her superiors. I use the same technique. For example, if asked to describe in writing my preferred teaching style, I might say, "I use direct and explicit instruction with worked examples to fulfill my intentionality of having students construct their own knowledge."

"What other PD did you have this year?" she asked.

"This is where it gets a bit difficult," I said. "I was required to attend a six-hour session held here at the school the week before school started."

"Why is this difficult?"

"Because I really didn't like it. It was called 'How to lesson design like a rock star teacher.' "

"It was about designing lessons?"

"More or less. I guess. I don't know. It was six hours of being all over the map, and the guy clearly didn't like certain things."

I stopped there. It was hard to know what to say or not say about it. There was the "ice breaker" in which the moderator—a jovial know-it-all who name-dropped several constructivist leaders he admired—had us state what our "super power" is? (Why is so much PD steeped with the vocabulary that has teachers being "rock stars" or "super heroes"?)

James, the union rep, said "Sarcasm," which I found interesting. When the leader got to me, I said, "Card magic." Although the moderator had a rejoinder for each person's response, he didn't know what to say to mine, so he moved on.

There was the comparison we had to make between various instructional methods, using a scoring rubric based on creativity, communication, collaboration, and critical thinking—a textbook example of confirmation bias. Creativity was based on whether the method incorporated open-ended questions with more than one answer. The moderator showed the first candidate on the screen:

My group agreed that there's nothing wrong with a math workbook and we gave it high points, but we didn't exactly follow the rubric either. We saw the need for practice and believed that not everything has to be open ended or collaborative. Because there are no wrong answers in situations like these, the moderator, upon seeing that we gave it a good score, exclaimed, "Good for you!" and then added "There's nothing wrong with workbooks; they have their place, but you have to be aware of the *potential* for creativity." Which was the edu-reform way of saying, "You really shouldn't have given workbooks such a high rating."

I told Ellen none of this given her educational inclinations.

"I can see that a six-hour session on lesson design is a bit much," she said. "But can you think of anything that you got out of it?" I could see she needed something positive in order to fill out her electronic form.

"Well, there was one thing that made sense," I said. "He was critical of projects like building models of the California missions out of sugar cubes, or making a model of a Navajo village, because it is not teaching anything other than the construction itself."

"Ah, good," she said and started typing. "How does this sound? 'Effective lessons should reflect and reinforce what students are expected to learn about a particular subject.'"

"Sounds good," I said.

I wasn't being completely honest about this part of the PD. I neglected to tell her that after making his point about how sugar cube missions had no educational value, he told us what he thought was in fact a good activity. (Wait for it.) "Minecraft!" he said.

For those who don't know, Minecraft is a video game version of Lego blocks in which players build structures while discovering and extracting raw materials, making tools, and fighting computer-controlled mobs.

I'm not sure what rubric he was using to give Minecraft high marks, but I suspect it had to do with the "potential" for creativity. Or words to that effect.

Chapter 16
INSTRUCTIONAL SHIFTS, FORMATIVE ASSESSMENTS, AND TAKING MATTERS INTO MY OWN HANDS

Whenever the phrase "instructional shifts" appears in an article about education, it is highly likely that what you're reading is blather, claptrap, drivel, garbage, and idiocy. (Sorry for all the adjectives; I was trying to avoid saying the word "crap.") It is even more so if the article talks about formative and summative assessments. Although formative assessment is a valid concept (particularly the work of Dylan Wiliam), as happens often in education it has become stripped of its original meaning and has become anything people want it to be.

For example, formative assessment may be defined as evaluating how someone is *learning* material (otherwise known as "checking for understanding") whereas summative assessments evaluate how much someone *has learned* (like quizzes or tests). The concept has basically evolved into "formative—good; summative—bad."

There are many ways to check for understanding, including asking questions, warm-ups, exit tickets, homework—even quizzes. Here's where it gets rather fuzzy. Some say summative assessments can be used formatively, by using the results to guide future instruction.

The overlapping nature of how these definitions have evolved gives me much cover in my quest to appear aligned with the edu-party line. My first parole officer, Ellen, got me started down the path of formative assessment. Although many of her suggestions were things I would never consider doing, there was one that I thought I'd try.

"Have you ever let students use their notes for a quiz or test?" she asked.

I liked the idea, and during my first year at Cypress I allowed my classes to use notes for quizzes but not tests. I believed that this would reinforce the idea of the value of notes. The problem was that some students' organizational skills were lacking—resulting in this typical conversation:

Student: How do you do this problem?

Me: Look in your notes.

Student: I can't find it.

Me: (Drawing a diagram on a mini-white board) How would you find the time each of the cars is driving?

Student: I don't know.

Me: (Writing "Distance = Rate × Time" underneath the diagram)

Student: Oh!

Such incidents led me to provide help to students in a direct manner rather than the "read my mind" approach that entails asking vague questions that serve to frustrate rather than elucidate. Sometimes I would partially work out the equation for a particular problem. Other times I would use an example of a similar problem. Expanding from a worked example to solve similar problems demands critical thought, and it does exactly what math reformers pretend that unguided discovery does.

I continued this approach with my Math 7 class during my second year at Cypress. I was intent on bolstering the confidence of my students who had suffered the previous year and were convinced they could not do math. I was making headway with them using JUMP, and I could see that getting decent test scores had positive results. But as we got into more complex topics, they were having difficulty and asking for help.

I knew that there was a potential that such an approach could quickly blossom into grade inflation and an artificial sense of achievement. So I justified my giving them help by telling myself, "Well, I guess this is a formative assessment and I'm using the results to guide future instruction." But I knew there were limits.

Diane was now my parole officer and I brought her up to speed on my formative assessment approach. "It's hard for me to not give help when I see they're on the wrong track," I told her during one of our sessions.

"Yes!" she said. "They have to learn from mistakes."

Fearing a foray into Jo Boaler's money-making "mistakes make your brain grow" motif, I rapidly changed the subject and tried out a new idea. "I've been thinking of giving students a choice when they ask how to do a problem or whether it's correct. If I answer, it will cost them points deducted from their score. I need to wean them from this dependence on my help."

"Brilliant!" she said.

And so I tried it. For the most part, it worked. Jimmy asked if a problem were correct and I said it would cost 5 points for me to answer. "Never mind," he said. For those students clearly lost, I would not deduct points. Over time it became a judgment call—do they really need help or just hand-holding?

I continued this technique and have used it at St. Stephens. It has evolved so that I will offer help as needed, but at a certain point in the school year I will announce my policy of deducting points for certain questions.

My algebra class at St. Stephens was a case in point. Most of the class stayed afloat and did well on tests and quizzes. But there were others who struggled and fell behind. I would offer hints and help for those who were clearly lost without deducting points. Some students would ask for help on tests and quizzes; some would not.

And then there was Lucy. Despite the one victory in which she was motivated enough to find a method for factoring more complex trinomials, she once again settled into her usual mode of angrily putting down answers that she thought made a kind of sense. In fact, I found that she had forgotten how to factor trinomials. She rarely asked for help during tests. I gave it to her anyway.

In keeping with summative assessments sometimes being formative, I advised her parents that it would be best if she repeated Algebra 1 in ninth grade. Lucy and her parents were receptive to this. There was one other student for whom I made the same recommendation and it was accepted, no question. Both went on to get *A*s in algebra their freshmen year.

My interpretation of formative and summative assessments may not be what others think it is. On the other hand, a friend who teaches English Language Arts told me she always called something "formative" that she didn't want to grade.

In the end, it all boils down to what used to be called "teaching."

Chapter 17
"MATH TALK," STALIN'S HEMORRHOIDS, AND A MURDER OF CROWS

The energy that accompanies the start of the school year begins to dwindle noticeably around Thanksgiving, continuing through the approach of Christmas. It starts up again for a short time in January. Around February or March, when the rains bring tree frogs, students (and teachers) start to sense that spring break is near, with summer vacation soon following.

Seventh graders are growing and starting to look like eighth graders. And eighth graders are now looking ahead and becoming nostalgic for what will soon be a big part of their past. It is a nostalgia in advance—a holding on to the familiar at the same time as saying goodbye.

In my Math 8 class at St. Stephens, the holding on to the familiar manifested itself in even more conversations than normal. The literature on math education does not talk much about eighth graders' conversations. I recently saw an article claiming that "research shows" that students who talk about their math thinking are motivated to learn. Another article said that "math talk" allows for deeper understanding through communication. In addition, this "math talk" is viewed as a form of formative assessment that gives teachers a peek into student thinking and where they need help.

To help students have a conversation there are certain cues they are taught to use, sometimes written on a poster in the room. These include prompts like "So Hallie is saying that...", "I disagree with Bob's solution because...", "After listening to Lynn I think the answer should be...", "Dave is right but I want to add..." and so on.

I believe that motivation comes from proper instruction, which allows students to carry out the tasks and achieve success. Math talk is an effective tool only if the instruction they received allows them to make use of it. Otherwise, it is like children dressing up in their parents' clothes to play "grownups."

For my Math 8 class, sometimes the conversations pertained to the math problems they were working on—and sometimes not. But as long as they were working on math, I didn't mind. Shortly after the tree frog incident when Jared tried unsuccessfully to find the loud croaker, I was putting my plan to teach them more algebra into high gear. I had introduced some simple factoring exercises, which Jared found fun—and he even said, "Invigorating!" as he did them.

We were making fairly good progress with factoring, but when we got to algebraic fractions they got a bit bogged down. I had to continually remind them to factor in order to simplify.

"I don't like factoring," Jared said.

"Why? You told me factoring problems were invigorating a few weeks ago."

"That was before they got complicated," he said.

His friend Kevin chimed in. "Factoring messes things up," he said.

"When you take algebra next year in high school, you will have seen all this already," I said. You'll be wondering why you thought this was difficult."

Mary and Valerie had their own private conversations, which would often merge with the others'. One particular conversation and its tributaries comes to mind. Valerie, avoiding saying the word "hell," said "H, E, double hockey sticks."

Lou reacted to this. "There's nothing wrong with saying the word 'hell.' It's a place," he said. Discussion followed about when "hell" was permissible to say and when it was not.

"I don't see the big deal," Lou said.

"You would if you were Catholic," Valerie said.

"Okay, I'm not Catholic, but I believe in Jesus. I just think Catholics are too strict about some things."

Kevin chimed in. "Well, this *is* a Catholic school so there are certain things you have to go along with."

"Hell shouldn't be one of them," Lou said, although it was unclear whether he meant the concept of hell itself or about saying the word.

Kevin then asked me how to find the lowest common denominator of two algebraic fractions. As I was showing him, Mary, who clearly did not want to do any more work, asked, "Lou, if I died would you cry at my funeral?"

"Well, I would be sad," he said. "But I don't cry easily."

"What would it take to get you to cry?" she asked.

He appeared to be in thought. "I don't know. When my grandmother died I didn't cry, but when my dog died, I did. I don't understand why."

I had finished helping Kevin with his problem, and thought I might help Lou with his. "You don't always cry when someone dies," I said. "When my mother died last summer I was sad but I didn't cry."

"Sorry about your mom," Valerie said.

The room grew suddenly quiet; students are listening when you least expect it.

"But then I had a dream about her one night," I said. "And when I was telling someone about the dream, I started crying."

"You probably cried because you knew you were saying goodbye," she said.

Which, unbelievably, was what the dream was about. I had to go somewhere but couldn't take my mother with me so I had to say goodbye. There was no need to mention that, so I didn't and conversations returned to less somber topics—in particular, the history paper Lou was writing about Stalin. "Stalin died from hemorrhoids," he said.

"How can you die from hemorrhoids?" I asked.

"From complications."

"I assume that will not be covered in your history paper," I said, but his answer was drowned out by a noisy chorus of crows in the tree outside.

"Can I chase the crows away?" Jared asked.

"Stay seated," I said and shut the door to the classroom.

"The door won't block out the sound," Jared said.

Once the door was shut, the crowing stopped. I said "Do you hear them now?"

Never at a loss for a rejoinder, Jared said, "The motion of the door scared them away."

"Do you have proof of that?" I asked.

He didn't answer.

"I'll take that as a no," I said.

"Can we play hangman?" Jared asked.

"If you're all finished with your math problems."

"There's only two minutes left of class," he said.

I gave the go-ahead, and Lou and Jared jumped up to put their hangman challenge on the board. I realized at that moment that I had grown quite fond of this class and that our little rituals were starting to feel like we were saying goodbye.

Chapter 18
AN UNEXPECTED NARRATIVE,
A LIMBIC DIALOGUE, AND A
NOTE FROM ELLEN

Having worked for forty years in both the private and public sectors prior to my retirement, I can say that the axiom I formulated in Chapter 14 applies to both the teaching and non-teaching worlds. Restated: "You never know for sure what's really going on, but general suspicions suffice to fit the narrative at hand until nuances prove otherwise."

I had kept my notice of termination at the Cypress School under wraps, having told only Diane and one teacher whom I trusted. I didn't want the students to know. I heard stories from other teachers about receiving layoff notices every year and getting hired back. Even the superintendent had said that it could be rescinded.

This bolstered a vague belief that the same would happen to me. I was therefore surprised when on a Monday in May, the teacher in whom I had confided said, "I'm sorry to hear you were let go."

Clinging to the narrative I had been given to understand, I said, "That can be rescinded."

She looked at me and, speaking rapidly, informed me of a new narrative. "Sandra has been told she will be replacing you."

This development had occurred the previous Friday; the whole school knew but me. Sandra, the third grade teacher, was told that she would be teaching my math classes the next year. They would be hiring a third-grade teacher to replace her.

My first thought before going into limbic mode was that at least I wasn't being replaced by Sandra's student teacher who had observed my algebra class the previous year. "Was anyone planning on telling me?"

"The principal is in her office," she said in very kind tones.

I took the hint and stormed into the principal's office. By way of greeting I said, "Well, I just heard that despite declining student enrollment, there's still going to be two math teachers and I'm not one of them. What the hell does this mean?"

"Yes, sometimes people are shuffled to make things come out right."

"Meaning what, exactly?" I asked.

The principal was a very nice woman who genuinely liked me but was not one to go against the superintendent. "Why don't we talk to the superintendent about this?" she suggested.

Entering his office in full limbic mode, I broke the ice.

"I have been more than professional about all of this and I am not happy that I am finding out from another teacher about Sandra taking over my job," I said. "Why wasn't I informed about this decision?"

"Do you think I have to share information about staff decisions?"

"Given that this affects me, I think that would be safe to say."

"Look, as I told you before, this had nothing to do with performance. I can't go against the law, though, and I had to let someone go. Since you were the least senior, it was you."

This reference to the law was interesting. I assumed he meant the law about the number of teachers in the face of declining enrollments. None of this made sense. Moving the more expensive Sandra into my spot, and hiring a third-grade teacher to replace her seemed like it didn't reduce the number of teachers.

The superintendent continued. "It's like in baseball," he said. "They let players go with trades all the time. It's the same here." I said nothing. "Look, you know I think highly of you. You've taught a tough class of seventh graders who really like you. I was even going to make you permanent."

This was true; he had told me that during my performance review. But something happened to make him change his mind. I knew I'd never know what it was. As he went on talking, I realized it was over for me and nothing was going to change.

My limbic mode having subsided I became professional once more, like a baseball player being traded. I told him I appreciated the opportunity to vent, because it would have festered had we not had the discussion.

Later as I was sitting in my classroom during lunch there was a knock on the door. It was Sandra. "I just want you to know that I had no idea you hadn't been told what happened. I feel terrible about it," she said. "And believe me, I really don't want to teach math. I want to stay teaching third grade. I was told that this is what I'm going to do."

"So you and James will be the math teachers?"

"Yes. We taught together before. I'll be teaching algebra. We'll both be teaching sixth grade because it's a big class." I could tell she felt bad about the situation. She said she was going to tell the principal she didn't want to teach math and to be kept in her position teaching third grade. I knew that nothing would change and it didn't.

I kept my silence about events; my students didn't know what happened. Over the next week, with the exception of James, teachers expressed their regrets. I notified Diane and Ellen. Diane said she would be happy to be a reference. And Ellen wrote me the following note:

"I am so sorry that you have had to endure this undeserved trauma. I have worked with new teachers for 20 years and have witnessed this process over and over again. Most of my teachers have gone on and taught at other schools and never looked back."

I had heard the same thing from other teachers I knew. One told me "Education is a crazy business. I would not expect you to be given a reason for being let go."

In a few weeks I would be hired by St. Stephens. In the meantime I found it oddly comforting to know that others had been through the same thing. Despite conflicting narratives about education, some things never change. And with that, I began the narrative of preparing my final exams.

CHAPTER 19
AN EVALUATION, THE RED BOOK,
AND CHECKING FOR UNDERSTANDING

Marianne, the principal at St. Stephens, would occasionally do informal observations of teachers without notice. I had such an observation about the second week of the school year during my Math 7 class. As she got seated at the desk she was greeted by John, one of my students hiding underneath.

"Sometimes they like to hide from me and surprise me," I said.

This sufficed as an explanation and gave her a window into how I run my classes. The lesson went well, and her written comments were positive. She made no mention of John hiding underneath the desk, but later in the day a teacher told me he heard about it, so apparently word gets around quickly.

A more formal evaluation occurred later in the school year. Prior to the event, I had to fill out a form outlining my plan, and among other things I was asked how I would "differentiate the lesson to meet the needs of all learners." This is one of those statements that teachers toeing the party line interpret as "Put the accommodation of weak students above any lesson goal you had in mind." I responded that I would give the stronger students more complex problems to do, although I wasn't sure whether that would occur in class or as part of their homework. But I felt my answer would pass muster.

The observation occurred in my algebra class on graphing quadratic functions. The students in that class were a noisy bunch and quite spontaneous. Earlier that year during a sudden downpour, the class cheered and before I could stop them, ran outside to get soaked in the rain, including Lucy, my recalcitrant student.

There was nothing to worry about for my evaluation; the students were well behaved and it wasn't raining. I had students come up and do graphing at the board as part of the lesson, I asked questions and called on those I knew would have answers, and then I called on weaker students who, I was glad to see, were able to answer as well.

After going through the lesson, I then assigned students to small groups. I did this to act in the manner that I assumed was expected of teachers aligned with the educational party line. I paired strong students with weaker ones and gave each group an equation to graph. I circulated around to answer questions and inspect what was done.

About a week later, I met with Marianne in her office, to go over her observations of that particular lesson. She handed me her written comments while she talked to me about her observation of my class.

"I really thought that was a good lesson," she said. "They followed the explanations, they were engaged, it was well-scaffolded, and it's clear that they really like you."

She offered me more praise, and it was obvious from this and previous conversations with her that she thought well of what I was doing. But evaluations being what they are, she then brought up her concerns.

"I notice that the textbook wasn't used in this lesson. How are you using it? Do you use it for homework?"

I wasn't sure what she was getting at here. I don't require students to have their books out while I teach, for one thing. But for another, I wasn't sure whether she was asking about my use of Dolciani's 1962 algebra textbook or the official textbook. So I proceeded cautiously. "The lesson was actually taken from the blue textbook," I said. (This is the official one.) "I incorporate problems from the book into my lesson, and yes, the homework is generally taken from the book."

I could see that she was concerned over whether we were adhering to the Common Core standards. I understood this—it would be bad for business if students graduating from St. Stephens would be at a disadvantage in public high schools. In her mind, sticking to the official textbook meant compliance with Common Core.

And while I had mentioned in my initial interview my extensive use of the Dolciani book in teaching algebra, and how I bought them off the internet, I discerned that such information had not stuck with her. So I offered further clarification which grew into an Abbot and Costello-like dialogue:

"I primarily use the book by Dolciani."

"The red book I've seen students with?"

"Yes. I dislike the blue book; I think Dolciani is much better."

"Do you use the blue book?"

"Yes; to cover what isn't addressed in Dolciani—like the lesson you saw, and pretty soon exponential functions."

"But you do use the red book?"

"Yes."

"So you're saying you use the red book as a supplement?" she asked.

I said "Yes" even though I believe we both knew that "supplant" would have been more accurate. But people hear what they want or need to hear.

Our conference ended positively, and afterward I read her written notes. She questioned how I checked for understanding, noting that I paired weaker students with stronger in my small groups. How I would assess whether the weaker could have completed the lesson without the stronger?

Excellent question; I had to agree. In acting the way I thought I was expected to act I hadn't implemented the small group motif as well as I could have. As far as how one checks for understanding, there are many ways—exit tickets, quizzes, random questions here and there. But sometimes you just have to say: "Well, judging by reactions and questions, by and large, they got it." When you're pretty far into the school year, you know which students serve as proxies.

She also noted that I did not do what I said I would in the pre-observation form; namely, give challenging problems to the stronger students. Her recommendation: "More intentionality to provide challenge to those students that need it."

There was that word again: "Intentionality." To be honest I forgot that I said I would do that. In the heat of teaching, we often forget our best intentions, although not intentionally.

She reiterated her concern about the textbook and recommended, "Intentional correlation between lesson and text to ensure Common Core standards need for Algebra 1 mastery are adequately covered." I'm fairly certain that our conversation assured her that the Common Core standards would be met. As far as my use of the "red book," I think she may have been saying that she would look the other way. Whether intentional or not, I cannot say.

Chapter 20
OUT ON GOOD BEHAVIOR,
AND A FINAL NARRATIVE

My meetings with Diane during my second year at Cypress had taken place once a week. During the last few weeks of meetings, we moved from the coffee shop ,which was proving to be too noisy, to my classroom.

The potential for ending our discussions reminded me of a conversation I had in the Math 7 class regarding how you cannot divide by zero, nor zero by zero. I asked about the latter. Someone said, "It's zero." I said, "Yes, that would be an answer." Someone else said "two," another said "seven," and others threw out numbers until I said, "There are lots of answers, which is why we call it indeterminate." I overheard Jimmy whispering to a classmate: "We could have kept this going for a long time."

This struck me as a fitting description of my talks—first with Ellen and then Diane—which, like the mathematical concept of zero divided by zero, seemed to be indeterminate. On the one hand, they were meant to help me be a better teacher. On the other, the discussions were often fueled by a chain of misconceptions and ideologies built on the magical thinking found in most ed schools. And they could go on for a long time.

The day finally came when all electronic checklists had been filled out and discussions ended.

The principal joined our final meeting, which Diane started by saying, "This has been quite a year for you. The seventh-grade class really gave you some challenges."

"Yes, they did," I said. "You can lead a horse to water, as they say. But I think some of them drank it."

"You weren't just leading them—you dragged them to the water. Kicking and screaming," she said. This was an exaggeration, of course, but it was in my favor so I let it go.

"Any words of wisdom for us on the mentoring process?" she asked.

I've had the "any words of wisdom" question asked of me by Human Resources people as part of exit interviews at other jobs I've had. It's one of those questions where they want to hear good things but are willing to take their lumps.

"I know we didn't always agree on things," I began.

"Yes," she said. "It's been interesting. You're certainly not what I expected when we first met."

Which was probably true. I'm definitely not someone in their twenties right out of ed school. And while I had successfully avoided getting into knock-down drag-outs about things like "productive struggle" and "differentiated instruction," I did feel bad about some of our disagreements and how I had expressed them.

"In any teaching situation, there are going to be people we don't agree with," I said with a bit of hesitation. I wasn't sure where this was going to end up—a not unfamiliar feeling for some of my math lessons.

"Maybe we don't agree with the way others teach or their philosophies about education. But somehow we all have to get along—we have to make it work,"

I went on. "And even though I disagreed with you on some things, there were things that I did agree with and which were helpful. So that's what I'm taking away from this."

Diane seemed pleased with what I said. I don't know if she viewed this as an apology. I suppose it was.

We then moved on to other business, signing papers, and getting instructions on how to retrieve my final teaching certificate from a certain website. And then a picture of me holding my certificate of completion.

And that was that.

I was now out on good behavior as a fully credentialed teacher, free to continue putting into practice my ideas about teaching math. Free, that is, to the extent possible with having to attend PD sessions that are about engagement but pretend to be about instruction. Or hearing teachers talk about particular students' learning styles. Or having discussions about how to instill students with a growth mindset, or being asked how I differentiate instruction in my classes, or being exhorted to engage students in productive struggle and, of course, having to be intentional.

I've been out on good behavior for over a year now and am tremendously happy at St. Stephens. As of this writing, I just completed my second year there. In keeping with my "We all have to get along" apology to Diane, I keep my views to myself. Most of the time anyway.

There is the occasional PD that I have to attend, but nothing as bad as what I've had to endure in the past. I hear teachers talk about blended learning and intentionality and growth mindsets now and then, but we all get along.

Getting along with others includes students as well as teachers. Which brings me to Lucy, my algebra student. It had been touch and go with her all year. During the final exam, she broke through her stubbornness and asked me for help. It was a point-slope problem, asking for the equation of a line passing through a point and which was perpendicular to a specific line.

"I don't know how to do this," she said. I allowed them to have one sheet of paper with any information they wanted on it. I pointed to the point-slope formula on her cheat sheet and she started working.

A few minutes later I came back to see how she was doing. She was crying.

"Oh, you're upset," I said. "What's the matter?"

She pointed to her answer to the problem.

"It's correct!" I said. "You got it right. Why are you upset?"

"But it doesn't make sense," she said.

I'm fairly sure she thought the problem was asking for an ordered pair of numbers. Getting an equation for an answer didn't fit her narrative, so to speak.

She finished the final and got a C in the class, and I'm pleased to say that she got As all the way through algebra the next year in ninth grade.

In an earlier chapter in which Lucy made an appearance, I alluded to how some may view me as someone who values procedure over understanding. While that may be the prevailing narrative with respect to the final exam episode above, I recognize that it may not be the only one. Therefore I offer a choice of narratives and nuances thereof that my readers may decide is most representative:

1. Understanding always trumps procedure.
2. Procedure always trumps understanding.
3. Procedure and understanding work in tandem. For some, the understanding will come later. For others, before. And for still others, never.
4. One should teach understanding but not obsess over it.

I've no doubt missed other narratives, but I'm somewhat new at this. I take a rather straightforward and un-nuanced view of the world. So I will leave it to you to add your own. Just don't tell me about them. I'm happy in my ignorance, and from what I hear from former students I'm doing just fine.

CPSIA information can be obtained
at www.ICGtesting.com
Printed in the USA
JSHW020508070322
23556JS00004B/5